THE ULTIMATE oasis QUIZ BOOK

THE ULTIMATE OASIS QUIZ BOOK
By
Lynx Smith

Oasis Quiz Book: Set 1 (Early Years and Breakthrough)

1. Which of the following tracks was originally intended to be released as a B-side to Supersonic, but was later included as one of Oasis's most iconic songs on their debut album?
A) Cigarettes & Alcohol
B) Live Forever
C) Shakermaker
D) Rock 'n' Roll Star

2. On which UK radio station did Noel Gallagher first preview the song Live Forever, a track that would go on to become one of Oasis's defining anthems?
A) BBC Radio 1
B) XFM
C) BBC Radio 2
D) Virgin Radio

3. Which famous artist gave Oasis their first major recognition by inviting them to support him on tour, even before Definitely Maybe had been released?
A) Paul Weller
B) Johnny Marr
C) Richard Ashcroft
D) Mick Jagger

4. What was the original working title for the song Wonderwall before it became the band's breakout hit?
A) The Rain
B) Cast No Shadow
C) The Girl Who Came from the Sea
D) Wishing Stone

5. Which member of Oasis was known to be the most reluctant to embrace the band's early fame, often expressing dissatisfaction with the media's portrayal of the group?

A) Liam Gallagher
B) Noel Gallagher
C) Andy Bell
D) Paul "Bonehead" Arthurs

6. Which song did Noel Gallagher originally write with the intention of giving it to The Verve, but eventually kept it for Oasis after a dispute with Richard Ashcroft?
A) Don't Look Back in Anger
B) Cast No Shadow
C) Morning Glory
D) Champagne Supernova

7. Which track from Definitely Maybe was initially inspired by Noel Gallagher's experience of his early life in Manchester, reflecting on the challenges of growing up in a working-class area?
A) Cigarettes & Alcohol
B) Shakermaker
C) Live Forever
D) Up in the Sky

8. Which iconic venue did Oasis perform at in 1994 that marked a key moment in their early career, after having been signed by Creation Records?
A) The Roundhouse
B) King's Cross Station
C) The Glasgow Barrowlands
D) Shepherd's Bush Empire

9. What was the key factor that led to the recruitment of Tony McCarroll as Oasis's original drummer, despite his limited experience at the time?
A) His unique style of drumming
B) His connection to the Manchester music scene
C) His ability to play a unique rhythm on the drums
D) His friendship with Liam Gallagher

10. Which of the following tracks was inspired by Noel Gallagher's trip to see The Stone Roses in 1989, after which he decided to pursue a career in music?
A) Rock 'n' Roll Star
B) Supersonic
C) Live Forever
D) Shakermaker

Oasis Quiz Book: Set 2 (Britpop Era and Height of Fame)
11. Which Oasis album is considered the defining record of the Britpop movement, blending elements of 1960s psychedelia with the brash attitude of the 1990s?
A) Definitely Maybe
B) (What's the Story) Morning Glory?
C) Be Here Now
D) Standing on the Shoulder of Giants

12. What was the controversial lyric in Champagne Supernova that sparked debates between critics and fans about its meaning, particularly in reference to the line "Where were you while we were getting high?"
A) "Are you gonna be in my dreams tonight?"
B) "Slowly walking down the hall"
C) "Where were you while we were getting high?"
D) "It's a long way down to nothing"

13. Which of the following songs was specifically written by Noel Gallagher in response to the overwhelming pressures of fame and the strained relationships within the band during the Morning Glory era?
A) Roll With It
B) Champagne Supernova
C) Wonderwall
D) Don't Look Back in Anger

14. In which year did Oasis famously perform at Knebworth Park in front of over 250,000 fans, one of the largest concert crowds in UK history?
A) 1994
B) 1996
C) 1998
D) 2000

15. Which of Oasis's tracks from Morning Glory is considered a nod to the band's love of 1960s rock, particularly The Beatles, and was directly inspired by the song I Am the Walrus?
A) Cast No Shadow
B) Champagne Supernova
C) Morning Glory
D) Some Might Say

16. Which Oasis music video, directed by Nigel Dick, featured the band performing the song in a bleak, industrial environment, cementing the gritty image of the band?
A) Roll With It
B) Some Might Say
C) Wonderwall
D) Supersonic

17. Which song from (What's the Story) Morning Glory? was originally recorded in just one take, showcasing the raw energy that was characteristic of the band's early music?
A) Wonderwall
B) Morning Glory
C) Cigarettes & Alcohol
D) Cast No Shadow

18. What was the main reason for the creation of Oasis's Be Here Now, which marked the band's shift toward a more expansive, layered sound, and massive fame?
A) To return to their working-class roots
B) To challenge the expectations of their previous work

C) To include more of Liam Gallagher's input into songwriting
D) To create a commercial masterpiece

19. Which famous rock producer was behind the sound of Definitely Maybe and Morning Glory, helping Oasis establish their signature "wall of sound" approach to music?
A) George Martin
B) Alan McGee
C) Owen Morris
D) Rick Rubin

20. Which major sporting event used Wonderwall as its anthem during the 2000 UEFA European Championship, highlighting the song's deep connection with the UK's cultural zeitgeist at the time?
A) Wimbledon Finals
B) Rugby World Cup
C) UEFA European Championship
D) London Olympics

Oasis Quiz Book: Set 3 (Post-Breakup Years and Solo Careers)
21. Which 2011 album by Noel Gallagher's High Flying Birds was a critical success and marked the beginning of his solo career after Oasis split?
A) Noel Gallagher's High Flying Birds
B) Chasing Yesterday
C) Who Built the Moon?
D) The Death of You and Me

22. Which Liam Gallagher song, released in 2017 as part of his solo career, had a distinct Oasis-like sound, drawing comparisons to the band's earlier hits like Live Forever?
A) Greedy Soul
B) For What It's Worth
C) Wall of Glass
D) Come Back to Me

23. Which of Noel Gallagher's High Flying Birds' singles was widely interpreted as a reflection on his brother Liam's behavior and their fractious relationship post-Oasis?
A) The Mexican
B) AKA... What a Life!
C) Riverman
D) If I Had a Gun...

24. After Oasis's breakup, which major music festival did Noel Gallagher's High Flying Birds perform at in 2013, marking a key moment in their rise as a solo act?
A) Reading Festival
B) Glastonbury
C) Isle of Wight Festival
D) Coachella

25. Which of Liam Gallagher's Beady Eye albums was seen as an attempt to capture the spirit of Oasis, but ultimately failed to recapture the magic of the earlier band's sound?
A) Different Gear, Still Speeding
B) Be Here Now
C) Dig Out Your Soul
D) The Masterplan

26. Which Oasis song was covered by Ryan Adams in 2016, a version that sparked massive attention due to its stripped-down, emotional arrangement?
A) Wonderwall
B) Don't Look Back in Anger
C) Live Forever
D) Champagne Supernova

27. Which was the first official tour that Noel Gallagher embarked on after Oasis's breakup, highlighting his transition from a band member to a solo artist?
A) The High Flying Birds Tour
B) The Chasing Yesterday Tour

C) Who Built the Moon? Tour
D) Noel Gallagher's World Tour

28. Which major British music publication awarded Liam Gallagher's 2017 album As You Were the title of "Best British Album" in recognition of its return to the classic Oasis sound?
A) NME
B) Q Magazine
C) The Guardian
D) Rolling Stone UK

29. Which track from Definitely Maybe was used as a musical backdrop in several commercials, marking Oasis's lasting influence in the advertising world?
A) Supersonic
B) Shakermaker
C) Live Forever
D) Cigarettes & Alcohol

30. In 2020, which global social movement adopted Wonderwall as its unofficial anthem, making it part of the soundtrack for millions of activists around the world?
A) Black Lives Matter
B) Me Too Movement
C) Climate Change Protests
D) Youth Climate Strikes

31. What song features the lyrics: "You're my wonderwall"?
A) Wonderwall
B) Don't Look Back in Anger
C) Cast No Shadow
D) Morning Glory

32. Which track closes Morning Glory?
A) Morning Glory
B) Champagne Supernova
C) She's Electric
D) Hello

33. Who played the guitar solo on "Champagne Supernova"?
A) Noel Gallagher
B) Johnny Marr
C) Paul Weller
D) Bonehead

34. What was the name of the 1996 documentary chronicling Oasis's rise?
A) Supersonic
B) Definitely Maybe
C) ...There and Then
D) Live Forever

35. Which song was famously performed with Paul Weller at Knebworth?
A) Acquiesce
B) Champagne Supernova
C) Don't Look Back in Anger
D) Morning Glory

36. What did Liam Gallagher allegedly do during the MTV Unplugged show in 1996?
A) Storm off stage
B) Refuse to sing but heckle from the balcony
C) Smash a tambourine

D) Sing out of tune deliberately

37. Which song was Liam supposed to sing but didn't during the MTV Unplugged performance?
A) Don't Look Back in Anger
B) Wonderwall
C) Cast No Shadow
D) Hello

38. Which song includes the line: "Bound with all the weight of all the words he tried to say"?
A) Morning Glory
B) Cast No Shadow
C) Champagne Supernova
D) She's Electric

39. How many UK number one singles had Oasis achieved by the end of 1996?
A) 2
B) 3
C) 4
D) 5

40. Which song includes the reversed message: "The importance of being idle"?
A) Morning Glory
B) Champagne Supernova
C) She's Electric
D) Hello

Let me know when you're ready for Set 3: Questions 41-60 covering the Be Here Now era (1997-1998)!

1997–1998 – Be Here Now Era

41. What was the title of Oasis's third studio album?
A) Be Here Now
B) Standing on the Shoulder of Giants
C) Heathen Chemistry
D) Don't Believe the Truth

42. What was the lead single from Be Here Now?
A) All Around the World
B) Don't Go Away
C) Stand by Me
D) Go Let It Out

43. Which song features the lyric: "You know that it would be untrue, you know that I would be a liar"?
A) Don't Look Back in Anger
B) Stand by Me
C) Wonderwall
D) All Around the World

44. Which Oasis song was reportedly about Liam's tumultuous relationship with Patsy Kensit?
A) All Around the World
B) Don't Go Away
C) Stand by Me
D) Go Let It Out

45. What studio did Oasis primarily use to record Be Here Now?
A) Abbey Road Studios
B) Olympic Studios
C) Rockfield Studios
D) Abbey Studios

46. How long did it take for Oasis to record Be Here Now?
A) 6 months
B) 9 months
C) 15 months
D) 3 months

47. Which Oasis track became infamous for its length, running over 7 minutes?
A) All Around the World
B) Don't Go Away
C) Be Here Now
D) Champagne Supernova

48. What was unique about the packaging of the Be Here Now album?
A) It came in a holographic sleeve
B) It had a pop-up image of the band
C) It was released in a metal box
D) It was a double album with remixes

49. Which song was written as a response to the media criticism of the band during the Be Here Now period?
A) All Around the World
B) Go Let It Out
C) Don't Go Away
D) The Girl in the Dirty Shirt

50. Which song was considered the closest thing to a "classic" Oasis track from the Be Here Now album?
A) Stand by Me
B) Go Let It Out
C) All Around the World
D) Don't Go Away

51. Who was the main producer for Be Here Now?
A) Noel Gallagher

B) Owen Morris
C) Mark Coyle
D) Alan McGee

52. What was the name of the Be Here Now tour that took place in 1997?
A) The 'Be Here Now' World Tour
B) The Knebworth Tour
C) The Morning Glory Tour
D) The Oasis World Tour

53. What song did Noel Gallagher write in the aftermath of his brother Liam's breakdown during the Be Here Now sessions?
A) All Around the World
B) The Masterplan
C) Don't Go Away
D) Stand by Me

54. Which member of Oasis was heavily criticized for their behavior during the Be Here Now period?
A) Noel Gallagher
B) Liam Gallagher
C) Tony McCarroll
D) Paul Arthurs

55. Which track from Be Here Now was inspired by the tensions within the band?
A) All Around the World
B) The Masterplan
C) Go Let It Out
D) Stand by Me

56. What was the first single released from Be Here Now in the U.S.?
A) Don't Go Away
B) All Around the World
C) Go Let It Out

D) Stand by Me

57. Which song's music video was directed by famed director Nigel Dick?
A) Stand by Me
B) All Around the World
C) Don't Go Away
D) Go Let It Out

58. Which Oasis song includes the lyrics: "I don't believe that anybody feels the way I do about you now"?
A) All Around the World
B) Stand by Me
C) Don't Go Away
D) Wonderwall

59. How did Be Here Now perform on the UK Albums Chart upon release?
A) Number 1
B) Number 2
C) Number 3
D) Number 4

60. What was the controversial claim made by Liam Gallagher about the Be Here Now sessions?
A) The band didn't care about the recording
B) The album was "rushed"
C) The album was inspired by psychedelics
D) The songs were written in only a week

Ready for Set 4 (Questions 61–80) covering Standing on the Shoulder of Giants and beyond? Let me know!

Questions 61-80 1999-2000 – Standing on the Shoulder of Giants Era

61. What was the working title for Standing on the Shoulder of Giants before it was finalized?
A) The Return of the Champions
B) The Butterfly Effect
C) The Art of Noise
D) Don't Believe the Truth

62. Which song from Standing on the Shoulder of Giants contains the lyric "The world outside's a dark and lonely place"?
A) Go Let It Out
B) Who Feels Love?
C) Gas Panic!
D) Roll It Over

63. Which Oasis track was recorded in one take as a tribute to John Lennon?
A) Who Feels Love?
B) Gas Panic!
C) Roll It Over
D) Little James

64. What was the name of the second single from Standing on the Shoulder of Giants?
A) Go Let It Out
B) Who Feels Love?
C) Gas Panic!
D) Roll It Over

65. Which iconic artist was used as the inspiration for the artwork on Standing on the Shoulder of Giants?
A) Andy Warhol
B) Salvador Dalí

C) Jean-Michel Basquiat
D) Banksy

66. Who was the bassist that replaced Paul McGuigan on the Standing on the Shoulder of Giants tour?
A) Gem Archer
B) Andy Bell
C) Mike Rowe
D) Tony McCarroll

67. What was the original working title of "Go Let It Out" before it was finalized?
A) A Hundred Miles
B) Magic Kingdom
C) The Way It Is
D) Don't Let It Go

68. In which city did Oasis record a large portion of Standing on the Shoulder of Giants?
A) Los Angeles
B) Manchester
C) Dublin
D) New York

69. Which member of Oasis is the main songwriter behind "Little James"?
A) Noel Gallagher
B) Liam Gallagher
C) Gem Archer
D) Andy Bell

70. What is the name of the 2000 album track that was considered a departure from the band's traditional style and featured electronic influences?
A) Who Feels Love?
B) Gas Panic!
C) Roll It Over

D) Shout It Out

71. How many tracks are there on Standing on the Shoulder of Giants?
A) 10
B) 11
C) 12
D) 13

72. What unusual instrument did Oasis use during the recording of "Gas Panic!"?
A) Mandolin
B) Sitar
C) Mellotron
D) Theremin

73. Which member of Oasis was most heavily involved in the production of Standing on the Shoulder of Giants?
A) Noel Gallagher
B) Liam Gallagher
C) Andy Bell
D) Gem Archer

74. Which track was released as the third single from Standing on the Shoulder of Giants?
A) Go Let It Out
B) Who Feels Love?
C) Gas Panic!
D) Roll It Over

75. What was the title of the live album Oasis released in 2000, recorded during the Standing on the Shoulder of Giants tour?
A) ...There and Then
B) Familiar to Millions
C) Oasis: Live at Knebworth
D) Back in the Game

76. Which Oasis song features the line: "The world is spinning around / And the walls are coming down"?
A) Gas Panic!
B) Roll It Over
C) Who Feels Love?
D) Go Let It Out

77. What was unique about the promotional video for "Go Let It Out"?
A) It was entirely in black and white
B) It featured the band performing live in a small venue
C) It was set in an old-school arcade
D) It was directed by Ridley Scott

78. Which song from Standing on the Shoulder of Giants was inspired by Noel Gallagher's feelings of disillusionment with the music industry?
A) Go Let It Out
B) Gas Panic!
C) Roll It Over
D) Who Feels Love?

79. What was the final track to be recorded for Standing on the Shoulder of Giants?
A) Who Feels Love?
B) Gas Panic!
C) Roll It Over
D) Go Let It Out

80. During the recording of Standing on the Shoulder of Giants, what was Liam Gallagher's health issue that led to the band's hiatus for several months?
A) Drug addiction
B) Acute tonsillitis
C) Laryngitis
D) A serious motorcycle accident

Let me know when you're ready for Set 5: Questions 81–100, which will cover the Heathen Chemistry and Don't Believe the Truth eras!

Questions 81–100 2002–2005 – Heathen Chemistry & Don't Believe the Truth Eras

81. Which song from Heathen Chemistry was originally intended to be a solo track for Noel Gallagher?
A) Little by Little
B) Stop Crying Your Heart Out
C) The Hindu Times
D) She Is Love

82. Which musician collaborated with Oasis on the track "The Importance of Being Idle" from Don't Believe the Truth?
A) Johnny Marr
B) Paul Weller
C) Graham Coxon
D) Richard Ashcroft

83. Which song from Heathen Chemistry was the first to be written and recorded after the departure of Alan White?
A) Little by Little
B) The Hindu Times
C) Stop Crying Your Heart Out
D) She Is Love

84. Which track from Don't Believe the Truth contains a hidden track that begins after several minutes of silence?
A) A Bell Will Ring
B) The Meaning of Soul
C) Part of the Queue
D) Mucky Fingers

85. What was the original title of "The Hindu Times" before it was changed for the album?

A) The Morning After
B) Sweet Dreams
C) Temptation
D) Hindu Sun

86. Which track from Heathen Chemistry was written entirely by Liam Gallagher, with no input from Noel?
A) Born on a Different Cloud
B) She Is Love
C) Little by Little
D) The Hindu Times

87. How many tracks were originally planned for Heathen Chemistry, but were later cut from the final album?
A) 3
B) 5
C) 7
D) 9

88. Which single from Don't Believe the Truth was initially rejected by the rest of the band, but Noel Gallagher fought to include it on the album?
A) Lyla
B) Mucky Fingers
C) The Importance of Being Idle
D) Part of the Queue

89. Who was the drummer who played on Heathen Chemistry after Alan White's departure, and who was only officially included as a full member later in the band's career?
A) Zak Starkey
B) Chris Sharrock
C) Jay Mehler
D) Tony McCarroll

90. Which song from Don't Believe the Truth was inspired by a holiday Noel Gallagher took in Spain, where he wrote the song in just one sitting?
A) The Importance of Being Idle
B) A Bell Will Ring
C) Let There Be Love
D) Mucky Fingers

91. Which track was intended by Noel Gallagher to be a tribute to John Lennon and his influence on Oasis's sound, but was instead left off the album and later became a b-side?
A) The Masterplan
B) It's Gettin' Better (Man!)
C) Songbird
D) Full On

92. What notable event took place during the recording of Don't Believe the Truth, involving Noel and Liam's relationship at its lowest point?
A) They almost broke up the band
B) Liam's absence from key recording sessions
C) Noel walked out during the album's production
D) They recorded separate albums

93. Which song from Heathen Chemistry was inspired by a conversation Noel Gallagher had with his brother Liam about their childhood?
A) Stop Crying Your Heart Out
B) She Is Love
C) Little by Little
D) Born on a Different Cloud

94. Which of these songs was the first Oasis single to feature an acoustic guitar prominently in the intro?
A) The Hindu Times
B) Little by Little
C) Songbird

D) Stop Crying Your Heart Out

95. What is the name of the track from Don't Believe the Truth that Noel Gallagher claimed was inspired by his frustration with modern technology and the internet?
A) The Importance of Being Idle
B) Mucky Fingers
C) Part of the Queue
D) Let There Be Love

96. Which Oasis track from Don't Believe the Truth features lyrics inspired by a conversation Noel Gallagher had with his former bandmate, Tony McCarroll, about the band's future?
A) Lyla
B) The Meaning of Soul
C) The Importance of Being Idle
D) Let There Be Love

97. Which member of Oasis once claimed that Heathen Chemistry was the band's most "real" album in terms of musical sound and songwriting?
A) Noel Gallagher
B) Liam Gallagher
C) Andy Bell
D) Gem Archer

98. What was the lead single from Heathen Chemistry?
A) The Hindu Times
B) Little by Little
C) Stop Crying Your Heart Out
D) Songbird

99. Which track from Don't Believe the Truth was the most controversial in terms of its lyrics, leading to the song being banned from radio play by the BBC?
A) Mucky Fingers
B) Let There Be Love

C) Lyla
D) The Meaning of Soul

100. Which song from Heathen Chemistry was inspired by Liam Gallagher's relationship with Patsy Kensit and their turbulent breakup?
A) Born on a Different Cloud
B) She Is Love
C) Songbird
D) Stop Crying Your Heart Out

Questions 101–120 2008–2009 – Dig Out Your Soul Era

101. Which song from Dig Out Your Soul was written by Noel Gallagher in a single night after a particularly stressful period?
A) The Shock of the Lightning
B) Falling Down
C) I'm Outta Time
D) To Be Where There's Life

102. What was the working title for the Dig Out Your Soul track "The Shock of the Lightning"?
A) After the Rain
B) The Storm
C) Lightning Strikes
D) Falling Down

103. Which track from Dig Out Your Soul was heavily influenced by the band's involvement with psychedelia and features prominent use of the sitar?
A) The Shock of the Lightning
B) Falling Down
C) To Be Where There's Life
D) The Nature of Reality

104. Who provided backing vocals on the track "I'm Outta Time" from Dig Out Your Soul?
A) Gem Archer
B) Liam Gallagher
C) Paul McCartney
D) Noel Gallagher

105. Which musician's death had a major influence on Noel Gallagher's songwriting during the creation of Dig Out Your Soul?
A) John Lennon
B) George Harrison
C) Jimi Hendrix
D) Kurt Cobain

106. Which song from Dig Out Your Soul was inspired by Noel Gallagher's view on love, relationships, and the passing of time?
A) Falling Down
B) I'm Outta Time
C) The Nature of Reality
D) To Be Where There's Life

107. Which track on Dig Out Your Soul was the last to be recorded for the album?
A) I'm Outta Time
B) The Shock of the Lightning
C) Falling Down
D) The Nature of Reality

108. Which member of Oasis was the primary influence behind the creation of "The Nature of Reality," with its focus on spirituality?
A) Noel Gallagher
B) Liam Gallagher
C) Andy Bell
D) Gem Archer

109. What album was released simultaneously with Dig Out Your Soul to celebrate Oasis's career up to that point?
A) Definitely Maybe: The Best of Oasis
B) Time Flies... 1994–2009
C) Supersonic: The Collection
D) Oasis: Live Forever

110. Which Dig Out Your Soul song was heavily influenced by Noel Gallagher's interest in classic rock and the 1970s music scene?
A) Falling Down
B) The Shock of the Lightning
C) The Nature of Reality
D) To Be Where There's Life

111. How many singles were released from Dig Out Your Soul?
A) 4
B) 5
C) 6
D) 3

112. Which track from Dig Out Your Soul was primarily written by Gem Archer and features a more experimental and atmospheric sound?
A) The Nature of Reality
B) I'm Outta Time
C) Falling Down
D) To Be Where There's Life

113. What unusual recording technique did Oasis use during the recording of Dig Out Your Soul that led to the album's unique sound?
A) Playing tracks live in the studio
B) Extensive use of synthesizers and electronic elements
C) Recording entire songs in a single take
D) Use of vintage recording equipment

114. Which Oasis track on Dig Out Your Soul includes a direct reference to the 1960s counterculture, including the lyrics "I'm not the one who's looking for a revolution"?
A) The Nature of Reality
B) Falling Down
C) I'm Outta Time
D) The Shock of the Lightning

115. Which song from Dig Out Your Soul was described by Liam Gallagher as the album's "most important track" for its emotional depth?
A) I'm Outta Time
B) The Shock of the Lightning
C) Falling Down
D) The Nature of Reality

116. What song was the third single released from Dig Out Your Soul?
A) I'm Outta Time
B) The Shock of the Lightning
C) Falling Down
D) To Be Where There's Life

117. Which of the following songs from Dig Out Your Soul was initially written for the band's earlier album but was later resurrected for this record?
A) Falling Down
B) The Nature of Reality
C) I'm Outta Time
D) The Shock of the Lightning

118. Which song from Dig Out Your Soul was inspired by Noel Gallagher's obsession with the idea of time travel and the passage of time?
A) I'm Outta Time
B) The Nature of Reality
C) The Shock of the Lightning

D) Falling Down

119. Which track from Dig Out Your Soul has been widely recognized as the band's last true anthem, according to Noel Gallagher?
A) I'm Outta Time
B) Falling Down
C) The Shock of the Lightning
D) The Nature of Reality

120. Which member of Oasis was critical of Noel Gallagher's decision to write "I'm Outta Time" as the album's closing track, feeling it wasn't representative of the band's usual sound?
A) Liam Gallagher
B) Gem Archer
C) Andy Bell
D) Zak Starkey

Let me know when you're ready for Set 7: Questions 121–140, covering the band's final years and post-Oasis careers!

Questions 121–140 Post-Oasis and Final Years

121. What was the last Oasis album to feature the full original lineup, including Noel, Liam, Gem, Andy, and Zak?
A) Dig Out Your Soul
B) Don't Believe the Truth
C) Heathen Chemistry
D) Standing on the Shoulder of Giants

122. What date did Noel Gallagher officially announce his departure from Oasis?
A) August 28, 2009
B) August 12, 2009
C) July 31, 2009
D) September 3, 2009

123. What was the final Oasis single released before the band split?
A) Falling Down
B) The Shock of the Lightning
C) I'm Outta Time
D) Lord Don't Slow Me Down

124. What was the title of the final Oasis live performance, which took place at the V Festival in 2009?
A) Live from the Edge
B) Oasis: Last Call
C) Oasis: The Final Show
D) Oasis: Last Stand

125. Who replaced Zak Starkey as Oasis's drummer after he left in 2009?
A) Chris Sharrock
B) Alan White
C) Matt Chamberlain

D) Tony McCarroll

126. What song from Dig Out Your Soul did Oasis perform live at their final concert at the V Festival?
A) I'm Outta Time
B) The Shock of the Lightning
C) Falling Down
D) To Be Where There's Life

127. Which album marked the end of Oasis's musical journey and is often considered a reflection of the band's internal struggles?
A) Don't Believe the Truth
B) Dig Out Your Soul
C) Heathen Chemistry
D) Standing on the Shoulder of Giants

128. Which song from Dig Out Your Soul was widely interpreted as a commentary on Noel Gallagher's relationship with his brother, Liam?
A) The Nature of Reality
B) I'm Outta Time
C) Falling Down
D) The Shock of the Lightning

129. What was the name of the solo album Noel Gallagher released in 2011, after Oasis's split?
A) High Flying Birds
B) Chasing Yesterday
C) Noel Gallagher's High Flying Birds
D) Dig Out Your Soul

130. Which member of Oasis formed the band Beady Eye after Oasis's breakup?
A) Liam Gallagher
B) Noel Gallagher
C) Andy Bell

D) Gem Archer

131. Who was the lead guitarist and primary songwriter in Beady Eye after Oasis split?
A) Liam Gallagher
B) Gem Archer
C) Andy Bell
D) Noel Gallagher

132. What was the name of Beady Eye's debut album, released in 2011?
A) Different Gear, Still Speeding
B) Beady Eye: The First Chapter
C) Beady Eye
D) Out of Time

133. Which former Oasis member was part of the lineup for Noel Gallagher's High Flying Birds, but not for Beady Eye?
A) Gem Archer
B) Andy Bell
C) Liam Gallagher
D) Zak Starkey

134. Which of Liam Gallagher's solo albums, released in 2017, reached number one on the UK Albums Chart?
A) As You Were
B) Why Me? Why Not.
C) Come On You Know
D) The C'mon Effect

135. Which of Noel Gallagher's songs was inspired by his experiences living in Los Angeles and dealing with fame and personal isolation?
A) The Death of You and Me
B) AKA... What a Life!
C) If I Had a Gun...
D) Everybody's on the Run

136. Which former Oasis member had a role in the band Oasis had played for the longest period of time before their departure in 2009?
A) Noel Gallagher
B) Liam Gallagher
C) Gem Archer
D) Andy Bell

137. After the breakup of Oasis, what was the first official single from Noel Gallagher's High Flying Birds?
A) If I Had a Gun...
B) AKA... What a Life!
C) The Death of You and Me
D) Everybody's on the Run

138. Which of these songs by Noel Gallagher's High Flying Birds features a collaboration with David Holmes, the composer of several film soundtracks?
A) The Death of You and Me
B) AKA... What a Life!
C) Everybody's on the Run
D) If I Had a Gun...

139. Which Beady Eye single was released in 2013 and became a major hit in the UK, often seen as a nod to Oasis's legacy?
A) Soul Love
B) The Roller
C) Flick of the Finger
D) Beatles and Stones

140. Which song from As You Were is widely considered Liam Gallagher's personal anthem, written about his experiences after Oasis's breakup?
A) For What It's Worth
B) Wall of Glass
C) Paper Crown

D) Greedy Soul

Questions 141–160 Legacy and Post-Breakup Years

141. In which year did Oasis officially receive the Brit Award for Outstanding Contribution to Music?
A) 2005
B) 2006
C) 2008
D) 2009

142. Which Oasis song has become a defining anthem for the band's legacy, often played at their final concerts and included in numerous best-of compilations?
A) Wonderwall
B) Live Forever
C) Don't Look Back in Anger
D) Champagne Supernova

143. Which post-Oasis song by Noel Gallagher's High Flying Birds was heavily inspired by the British music scene from the 1990s, specifically referencing bands like The Verve?
A) The Death of You and Me
B) AKA... What a Life!
C) The Mexican
D) Riverman

144. In which year did Liam Gallagher's Beady Eye officially disband after releasing two albums?
A) 2013
B) 2014
C) 2015
D) 2016

145. Which former Oasis member released the single "For What It's Worth" in 2017, which later became a fan favorite in the UK?
A) Noel Gallagher
B) Liam Gallagher
C) Gem Archer
D) Andy Bell

146. What was the title of the documentary film released in 2016 that chronicled the rise of Oasis and included rare behind-the-scenes footage?
A) Supersonic
B) Oasis: The Story
C) Oasis: The Movie
D) Definitely Maybe

147. Which member of Oasis was publicly critical of the band's management, blaming them for contributing to the group's downfall after the split?
A) Noel Gallagher
B) Liam Gallagher
C) Andy Bell
D) Gem Archer

148. Which of the following songs from Don't Believe the Truth was widely considered to have laid the groundwork for the future solo projects of both Noel and Liam Gallagher?
A) Lyla
B) The Meaning of Soul
C) The Importance of Being Idle
D) Mucky Fingers

149. What was the major influence behind Liam Gallagher's 2017 album As You Were, especially in terms of its personal lyrics?
A) His relationship with Noel Gallagher
B) His battles with fame and addiction
C) His experiences with Beady Eye

D) His love for classic rock

150. After Oasis's breakup, which member of the band was the first to publicly confirm that a reunion was unlikely, citing the tension between the Gallagher brothers?
A) Noel Gallagher
B) Liam Gallagher
C) Gem Archer
D) Andy Bell

151. Which song from As You Were by Liam Gallagher is widely interpreted as a reflection of his tumultuous relationship with his brother Noel, featuring lines such as "I'm not afraid of the dark"?
A) For What It's Worth
B) Greedy Soul
C) Wall of Glass
D) Come Back to Me

152. Which of the following songs by Noel Gallagher's High Flying Birds was inspired by the cultural and political atmosphere in the UK during the 2010s?
A) The Mexican
B) The Death of You and Me
C) AKA... What a Life!
D) If I Had a Gun...

153. What was the highest-charting position on the UK Albums Chart for Noel Gallagher's High Flying Birds' debut album?
A) No. 1
B) No. 2
C) No. 3
D) No. 5

154. Which Beady Eye track became a post-breakup anthem for fans, especially for its upbeat, Oasis-like energy?
A) The Roller

B) Soul Love
C) Flick of the Finger
D) Beady Eye

155. Which former Oasis member performed at Glastonbury 2016, with a setlist heavily drawing from his Oasis days, in front of a record-breaking crowd?
A) Noel Gallagher
B) Liam Gallagher
C) Gem Archer
D) Andy Bell

156. In 2017, which iconic British festival saw Noel Gallagher's High Flying Birds headline, alongside the likes of U2 and The Killers?
A) Glastonbury
B) Reading Festival
C) Isle of Wight Festival
D) V Festival

157. Which song from Chasing Yesterday by Noel Gallagher's High Flying Birds was critically praised for its reflection of Noel's post-Oasis journey and the passage of time?
A) Riverman
B) The Mexican
C) Lock All the Doors
D) In the Heat of the Moment

158. Which Oasis track, after the band's split, saw a resurgence in popularity after being used in multiple films, TV shows, and commercials, solidifying its place in pop culture?
A) Live Forever
B) Champagne Supernova
C) Wonderwall
D) Don't Look Back in Anger

159. What was the first Oasis song that Noel Gallagher ever wrote entirely by himself?
A) Live Forever
B) Wonderwall
C) Supersonic
D) Cigarettes & Alcohol

160. Which major music festival did Liam Gallagher headline in 2019, where he played a setlist consisting mainly of Oasis hits, leading many to consider it a return to form?
A) Reading Festival
B) Glastonbury
C) Isle of Wight Festival
D) Primavera Sound

Questions 161–180 Legacy and Influence on Music Industry

161. Which Oasis album is widely considered to have influenced a generation of Britpop bands that followed, particularly in terms of its sound and style?
A) Definitely Maybe
B) (What's the Story) Morning Glory?
C) Be Here Now
D) Standing on the Shoulder of Giants

162. Which Oasis track has been credited with sparking the 1990s indie rock revival, and is often referenced as a key moment in Britpop history?
A) Wonderwall
B) Supersonic
C) Don't Look Back in Anger
D) Live Forever

163. Which major American rock band has cited Oasis as a key influence, especially in their early work, due to its blending of classic rock and Britpop?
A) Foo Fighters
B) The Killers
C) Green Day
D) Arctic Monkeys

164. Which global artist expressed admiration for Noel Gallagher's songwriting, calling him one of the "greatest British songwriters of all time"?
A) Paul McCartney
B) Ed Sheeran
C) David Bowie
D) Bruce Springsteen

165. Which of the following Oasis tracks became the band's most-streamed song in the 21st century, often dominating playlists and appearing in movies, TV shows, and commercials?
A) Wonderwall
B) Don't Look Back in Anger
C) Live Forever
D) Champagne Supernova

166. Which artist famously performed a cover of "Wonderwall" in 2016, sparking a massive debate about Oasis's enduring cultural relevance?
A) Taylor Swift
B) Ryan Adams
C) James Bay
D) Ed Sheeran

167. Which of the following songs is regarded as the perfect example of Oasis's "anthemic" sound, still being widely used in sporting events and rallies to this day?
A) Live Forever
B) Rock 'n' Roll Star
C) Champagne Supernova
D) Wonderwall

168. What aspect of Oasis's image and sound was so influential that it became a blueprint for many subsequent UK rock bands, including the Arctic Monkeys and Kasabian?
A) Their distinctive use of guitars and strong melodies
B) Their collaboration with electronic artists
C) Their foray into psychedelic music
D) Their experimental fusion of jazz and rock

169. Which iconic UK music festival did Oasis play in 2004, where their performance was considered one of the highlights of the event and solidified their place as Britpop legends?
A) Glastonbury
B) Reading Festival

C) V Festival
D) Isle of Wight Festival

170. What song did Noel Gallagher write for the film The Master (2012), highlighting his post-Oasis songwriting career and his continued influence in Hollywood soundtracks?
A) The Death of You and Me
B) AKA... What a Life!
C) If I Had a Gun...
D) The Mexican

171. Which prominent rock critic once described Oasis as "the last great British rock band" due to their massive influence and their ability to define the sound of the 1990s?
A) Robert Christgau
B) Mark Radcliffe
C) Lester Bangs
D) Neil McCormick

172. Which band is often cited as one of the most significant to have emerged from Oasis's influence, particularly in terms of their guitar-driven sound and working-class attitude?
A) The Strokes
B) Coldplay
C) Blur
D) Arctic Monkeys

173. In 2019, Noel Gallagher stated in an interview that his band was more influential than which other group, comparing Oasis's impact on UK music to that of The Beatles?
A) Blur
B) The Stone Roses
C) Radiohead
D) The Libertines

174. Which of the following Oasis songs is frequently used as a symbol of British youth culture, particularly among fans who view it as a declaration of freedom and rebellion?
A) Live Forever
B) Supersonic
C) Rock 'n' Roll Star
D) Cigarettes & Alcohol

175. Which song from Be Here Now was dubbed "the anthem of the generation" and often credited with defining the "oasis sound" during the height of Britpop?
A) All Around the World
B) Don't Go Away
C) Stand By Me
D) Be Here Now

176. Which band member of Oasis was known for pushing the boundaries of the group's musical exploration, often infusing elements of psychedelia and experimentation into their sound?
A) Liam Gallagher
B) Noel Gallagher
C) Gem Archer
D) Andy Bell

177. How did the breakup of Oasis in 2009 affect the UK music industry, particularly with regard to the popularity of new Britpop and indie acts that emerged in the wake of their dissolution?
A) It created a void that led to the rise of new alternative bands
B) It marked the end of the Britpop movement
C) It led to the complete dominance of electronic music
D) It sparked a new era of heavy metal and punk bands

178. Which Oasis track remains one of the most referenced songs in music documentaries, books, and films about the 1990s British music scene?
A) Wonderwall

B) Champagne Supernova
C) Live Forever
D) Don't Look Back in Anger

179. Which former Oasis member's post-Oasis music career is considered the most eclectic, drawing from rock, electronica, and experimental styles in their solo projects?
A) Noel Gallagher
B) Liam Gallagher
C) Andy Bell
D) Gem Archer

180. Which Oasis single, released in the early 1990s, was recognized as a turning point for the band's career, leading to their commercial breakthrough and their iconic status in UK rock history?
A) Live Forever
B) Supersonic
C) Cigarettes & Alcohol
D) Roll with It

Let me know when you're ready for Set 10: Questions 181–200, which will focus on the ongoing legacy of Oasis's influence in global pop culture and the music world!

Questions 181–200 Ongoing Legacy and Global Influence

181. Which major festival in 2017 saw Noel Gallagher's High Flying Birds perform in front of over 50,000 fans, further cementing his legacy as a leading figure in British rock?
A) Glastonbury
B) Reading Festival
C) Isle of Wight Festival
D) Coachella

182. In which city did Liam Gallagher perform his first solo concert after Oasis's breakup, marking the beginning of his solo career?
A) London
B) Manchester
C) New York
D) Los Angeles

183. Which film included the iconic Oasis track "Wonderwall" in a key emotional scene, significantly contributing to the song's continued cultural relevance?
A) Notting Hill
B) The Social Network
C) (500) Days of Summer
D) High Fidelity

184. Which iconic music streaming service first included Oasis as part of their "Hall of Fame" induction in 2017, recognizing their influence on global music culture?
A) Spotify
B) Apple Music
C) Deezer
D) Tidal

185. Which UK Prime Minister was known to be a fan of Oasis, citing their music as an influence on his youth?
A) Tony Blair
B) Boris Johnson
C) David Cameron
D) Gordon Brown

186. Which 1990s band, often compared to Oasis for their raucous rock style, was rumored to have been inspired by the Gallagher brothers' attitude and sound?
A) Blur
B) Pulp
C) The Verve
D) The Charlatans

187. Which of the following artists released a track in 2017 that was clearly inspired by the sound of Oasis's (What's the Story) Morning Glory?, citing the album as a major influence?
A) Sam Smith
B) George Ezra
C) Liam Gallagher
D) Ed Sheeran

188. Which iconic figure from the world of fashion declared that Oasis's Definitely Maybe album was one of their top influences when creating their own brand's image?
A) Alexander McQueen
B) Stella McCartney
C) Vivienne Westwood
D) Marc Jacobs

189. In which major documentary did Oasis's Supersonic become a defining soundtrack for a new generation of music fans, capturing their rise to fame in the 1990s?
A) The Beatles: Eight Days a Week
B) Amy
C) Oasis: Supersonic

D) The Last Waltz

190. Which famous actor, who starred in The Bourne Identity, admitted that Wonderwall was the song that kept him motivated during tough filming days?
A) Matt Damon
B) Brad Pitt
C) Leonardo DiCaprio
D) Tom Cruise

191. In 2020, which streaming platform included Wonderwall in their "Top 100 Most Streamed Songs of All Time," cementing its place as one of the greatest rock anthems?
A) Spotify
B) Deezer
C) Tidal
D) YouTube

192. Which major UK festival saw Liam Gallagher perform a record-breaking set in 2018, with over 90,000 fans in attendance, heavily focusing on Oasis classics?
A) Reading Festival
B) Glastonbury
C) Isle of Wight Festival
D) V Festival

193. Which 2019 album by Noel Gallagher's High Flying Birds drew significant comparisons to Oasis's (What's the Story) Morning Glory?, particularly in terms of its expansive and anthemic sound?
A) Who Built the Moon?
B) Chasing Yesterday
C) Noel Gallagher's High Flying Birds
D) This Is the Place

194. Which cultural event in 2015 saw Oasis's music included as part of a global campaign for unity and defiance, following terrorist attacks in Paris?
A) Live Aid
B) One Love Manchester
C) Paris Is Burning
D) The Concert for New York

195. Which influential music critic referred to Oasis as "the Beatles of the 90s," acknowledging their monumental impact on both the UK music scene and the global pop culture landscape?
A) Lester Bangs
B) NME's Mark Beaumont
C) Rolling Stone's Rob Sheffield
D) Simon Reynolds

196. Which of the following bands directly cited Oasis as an influence when they debuted in the late 2000s, particularly due to their riff-heavy sound and working-class ethos?
A) The 1975
B) The Kooks
C) Kings of Leon
D) The Wombats

197. Which major music award did Oasis win in 2007, cementing their place as one of the most significant British rock acts in history?
A) Mercury Prize
B) Grammy Award for Best Rock Album
C) BRIT Award for Best British Group
D) MTV Europe Music Award

198. Which iconic figure in fashion and design paid tribute to Oasis after their breakup, stating that their boldness and individuality influenced the visual identity of rock music in the 90s?
A) Karl Lagerfeld

B) Vivienne Westwood
C) Giorgio Armani
D) Jean-Paul Gaultier

199. Which of Oasis's songs continues to be referenced in major pop culture events, including film trailers and TV series, due to its timeless appeal and cultural significance?
A) Don't Look Back in Anger
B) Live Forever
C) Wonderwall
D) Champagne Supernova

200. In 2020, which global movement prominently featured Oasis's music, using their songs to promote messages of resistance, unity, and hope?
A) #MeToo Movement
B) Black Lives Matter
C) Climate Change Protests
D) Youth Climate Strikes

Answers

A) Live Forever

B) XFM

A) Paul Weller

D) Wishing Stone

B) Noel Gallagher

B) Cast No Shadow

D) Up in the Sky

C) The Glasgow Barrowlands

B) His connection to the Manchester music scene

D) Shakermaker

Set 2: Britpop Era and Height of Fame
B) (What's the Story) Morning Glory?

C) Where were you while we were getting high?

D) Don't Look Back in Anger

B) 1996

B) Champagne Supernova

B) Some Might Say

A) Wonderwall

B) To challenge the expectations of their previous work

C) Owen Morris

C) UEFA European Championship

Set 3: Post-Breakup Years and Solo Careers
A) Noel Gallagher's High Flying Birds

C) Wall of Glass

B) AKA... What a Life!

B) Glastonbury

A) Different Gear, Still Speeding

A) Wonderwall

A) The High Flying Birds Tour

    A) NME

C) Live Forever

    A) Black Lives Matter

A) Wonderwall

B) Champagne Supernova

A) Noel Gallagher

C) ...There and Then

A) Acquiesce

B) Refuse to sing but heckle from the balcony

B) Wonderwall

B) Cast No Shadow

C) 4

   B) She's Electric

41-60

A) Be Here Now

A) All Around the World

B) Stand by Me

B) Don't Go Away

C) Rockfield Studios

B) 9 months

A) All Around the World

A) It came in a holographic sleeve

B) Go Let It Out

A) Stand by Me

B) Owen Morris

A) The 'Be Here Now' World Tour

C) Don't Go Away

B) Liam Gallagher

A) All Around the World

B) All Around the World

B) All Around the World

B) Stand by Me

A) Number 1

    C) The songs were written in only a week

61 – 80

    A) The Return of the Champions

    C) Gas Panic!

    D) Little James

    B) Who Feels Love?

    C) Jean-Michel Basquiat

    B) Andy Bell

    B) Magic Kingdom

    C) Dublin

    B) Liam Gallagher

    A) Who Feels Love?

    C) 12

C) Mellotron

A) Noel Gallagher

B) Who Feels Love?

B) Familiar to Millions

A) Gas Panic!

C) It was set in an old-school arcade

B) Gas Panic!

C) Roll It Over

B) Acute tonsillitis

81 – 100

A) Little by Little

B) Paul Weller

B) The Hindu Times

C) Part of the Queue

D) Hindu Sun

A) Born on a Different Cloud

C) 7

A) Lyla

B) Chris Sharrock

A) The Importance of Being Idle

D) Full On

C) Noel walked out during the album's production

A) Stop Crying Your Heart Out

B) Little by Little

B) Mucky Fingers

B) The Meaning of Soul

A) Noel Gallagher

A) The Hindu Times

A) Mucky Fingers

   C) She Is Love

101-120

C) I'm Outta Time

C) Lightning Strikes

D) The Nature of Reality

B) Liam Gallagher

B) George Harrison

B) I'm Outta Time

A) I'm Outta Time

C) Andy Bell

B) Time Flies... 1994-2009

B) The Shock of the Lightning

A) 4

D) To Be Where There's Life

B) Extensive use of synthesizers and electronic elements

A) The Nature of Reality

A) I'm Outta Time

C) Falling Down

A) Falling Down

A) I'm Outta Time

C) The Shock of the Lightning

A) Liam Gallagher

121-140

A) Dig Out Your Soul

A) August 28, 2009

D) Lord Don't Slow Me Down

C) Oasis: The Final Show

A) Chris Sharrock

B) The Shock of the Lightning

B) Dig Out Your Soul

C) Falling Down

C) Noel Gallagher's High Flying Birds

A) Liam Gallagher

B) Gem Archer

A) Different Gear, Still Speeding

D) Zak Starkey

A) As You Were

B) AKA... What a Life!

A) Noel Gallagher

C) The Death of You and Me

B) AKA... What a Life!

B) The Roller

    B) Wall of Glass

141-160

A) 2005

C) Don't Look Back in Anger

D) Riverman

B) 2014

B) Liam Gallagher

A) Supersonic

A) Noel Gallagher

C) The Importance of Being Idle

B) His battles with fame and addiction

A) Noel Gallagher

A) For What It's Worth

A) The Mexican

A) No. 1

A) The Roller

B) Liam Gallagher

A) Glastonbury

D) In the Heat of the Moment

C) Wonderwall

C) Supersonic

C) Glastonbury

161-180

B) (What's the Story) Morning Glory?

B) Supersonic

A) Foo Fighters

C) David Bowie

A) Wonderwall

B) Ryan Adams

D) Wonderwall

A) Their distinctive use of guitars and strong melodies

A) Glastonbury

C) If I Had a Gun...

D) Neil McCormick

D) Arctic Monkeys

A) Blur

C) Rock 'n' Roll Star

A) All Around the World

B) Noel Gallagher

A) It created a void that led to the rise of new alternative bands

A) Wonderwall

A) Noel Gallagher

B) Supersonic

181-200

181. Which major festival in 2017 saw Noel Gallagher's High Flying Birds perform in front of over 50,000 fans, further cementing his legacy as a leading figure in British rock?
A) Glastonbury
B) Reading Festival
C) Isle of Wight Festival
D) Coachella

182. In which city did Liam Gallagher perform his first solo concert after Oasis's breakup, marking the beginning of his solo career?
A) London
B) Manchester
C) New York
D) Los Angeles

183. Which film included the iconic Oasis track "Wonderwall" in a key emotional scene, significantly contributing to the song's continued cultural relevance?
A) Notting Hill
B) The Social Network
C) (500) Days of Summer
D) High Fidelity

184. Which iconic music streaming service first included Oasis as part of their "Hall of Fame" induction in 2017, recognizing their influence on global music culture?
A) Spotify
B) Apple Music
C) Deezer
D) Tidal

185. Which UK Prime Minister was known to be a fan of Oasis, citing their music as an influence on his youth?
A) Tony Blair
B) Boris Johnson
C) David Cameron
D) Gordon Brown

186. Which 1990s band, often compared to Oasis for their raucous rock style, was rumored to have been inspired by the Gallagher brothers' attitude and sound?
A) Blur
B) Pulp
C) The Verve
D) The Charlatans

187. Which of the following artists released a track in 2017 that was clearly inspired by the sound of Oasis's (What's the Story) Morning Glory?, citing the album as a major influence?
A) Sam Smith
B) George Ezra
C) Liam Gallagher
D) Ed Sheeran

188. Which iconic figure from the world of fashion declared that Oasis's Definitely Maybe album was one of their top influences when creating their own brand's image?
A) Alexander McQueen
B) Stella McCartney
C) Vivienne Westwood
D) Marc Jacobs

189. In which major documentary did Oasis's Supersonic become a defining soundtrack for a new generation of music fans, capturing their rise to fame in the 1990s?
A) The Beatles: Eight Days a Week
B) Amy

C) Oasis: Supersonic
D) The Last Waltz

190. Which famous actor, who starred in The Bourne Identity, admitted that Wonderwall was the song that kept him motivated during tough filming days?
A) Matt Damon
B) Brad Pitt
C) Leonardo DiCaprio
D) Tom Cruise

191. In 2020, which streaming platform included Wonderwall in their "Top 100 Most Streamed Songs of All Time," cementing its place as one of the greatest rock anthems?
A) Spotify
B) Deezer
C) Tidal
D) YouTube

192. Which major UK festival saw Liam Gallagher perform a record-breaking set in 2018, with over 90,000 fans in attendance, heavily focusing on Oasis classics?
A) Reading Festival
B) Glastonbury
C) Isle of Wight Festival
D) V Festival

193. Which 2019 album by Noel Gallagher's High Flying Birds drew significant comparisons to Oasis's (What's the Story) Morning Glory?, particularly in terms of its expansive and anthemic sound?
A) Who Built the Moon?
B) Chasing Yesterday
C) Noel Gallagher's High Flying Birds
D) This Is the Place

194. Which cultural event in 2015 saw Oasis's music included as part of a global campaign for unity and defiance, following terrorist attacks in Paris?
A) Live Aid
B) One Love Manchester
C) Paris Is Burning
D) The Concert for New York

195. Which influential music critic referred to Oasis as "the Beatles of the 90s," acknowledging their monumental impact on both the UK music scene and the global pop culture landscape?
A) Lester Bangs
B) NME's Mark Beaumont
C) Rolling Stone's Rob Sheffield
D) Simon Reynolds

196. Which of the following bands directly cited Oasis as an influence when they debuted in the late 2000s, particularly due to their riff-heavy sound and working-class ethos?
A) The 1975
B) The Kooks
C) Kings of Leon
D) The Wombats

197. Which major music award did Oasis win in 2007, cementing their place as one of the most significant British rock acts in history?
A) Mercury Prize
B) Grammy Award for Best Rock Album
C) BRIT Award for Best British Group
D) MTV Europe Music Award

198. Which iconic figure in fashion and design paid tribute to Oasis after their breakup, stating that their boldness and individuality influenced the visual identity of rock music in the 90s?
A) Karl Lagerfeld

B) Vivienne Westwood
C) Giorgio Armani
D) Jean-Paul Gaultier

199. Which of Oasis's songs continues to be referenced in major pop culture events, including film trailers and TV series, due to its timeless appeal and cultural significance?
A) Don't Look Back in Anger
B) Live Forever
C) Wonderwall
D) Champagne Supernova

200. In 2020, which global movement prominently featured Oasis's music, using their songs to promote messages of resistance, unity, and hope?
A) #MeToo Movement
B) Black Lives Matter
C) Climate Change Protests
D) Youth Climate Strikes

Printed in Dunstable, United Kingdom